The Secret of Sugar Water

With love,
Feminista Jones

The Secret of Sugar Water

Written by Feminista Jones

PIAH
Publishing

PIAH Publishing
Philadelphia, PA 2017

For Garvey, my greatest love.

I'm not a poet.

I'm something like a conduit.

Words may be poetry's greatest obstacle.
The human mind restricts understanding.
Our relatively limited comprehension of life denies
poetry its full potential.

That's just kinda how it goes.
Here I am, sharing what some might call poetry. I
wrote these pieces over several years, beginning in
2004. From motherhood to protest, from love to
Blackness, these poems capture so much of who I
am while only scratching the surface of what I think
I understand.

I hope some of it connects with you.

XOXO,

The Secret of Sugar Water

I offer a glass of cool water
When you seek relief
On a hot day, one of many
And I watch you drain my cup
In one greedy gulp
You then demand another
Exasperated
Wondering why I am not already poised
To pour you another
"I'm thirsty!" you cry
And I know better than to laugh
I pour you another
Cool glass of sugar water
And I watch you, again, drain my cup
You wipe your brow
Put your hand to your eyes to block the glare of the sun
And you say
"This is the best water I've ever drank"
I say, "It's nothing but sugar water"
You pause and pick up my cup
And ask,
"What's the secret of sugar water?"
I pause and look down at you
And say,
"It's sugar and water"
You stare at my cup in disbelief

"What do you mean?" you ask
Unable to comprehend the simplicity
"The recipe is easy. It's a half cup of sugar
And eight ounces of water"
You make a mental note
And leave my table without gratitude
In your own home, your children moan with thirst
So, you pour half a cup of sugar
And eight ounces of water
And offer them relief
When they drink, they gag
And spit it out
"This is disgusting!" your youngest complains
You don't understand
After sipping your own brew, you spit it out
Gagging, you slam your cup down
Believing you've been deceived
So, you come back to me
Because you can't help your own children
You ask, again
"What's the secret of sugar water?"
I stare at you, trying not to laugh
And hide my disdain
"It's a half cup of sugar
And eight ounces of water"
Your balled-up fists reveal your simmering rage
You pound my table, demanding another answer
Because it didn't work for you

You blame me
Because you can't ease your children's suffering
You storm through my kitchen
Open and slam my cupboard doors
You examine my water
The same as yours
"You're lying!"
I laugh
"You're hiding!"
I stop
You stand before me, pleading
"Please! Tell me the secret of sugar water!
My children are dying of thirst and the only relief
Is in your secret
When I tried it myself
I couldn't make it work
Surely, you have some secret ingredient
That makes it just right
For your own children!"
Your fear fills the space of my small kitchen
Grabbing my pitcher, half empty by now
"I'm taking this for my own children" you say
"Take whatever you need"
"And I'll be coming back tomorrow for more"
You leave, again without a word of thanks
I make a new pitcher
For my children
Then I make another pitcher of sugar water

For you and yours

Blue

The blues ain't nothing but a
Song my people sing
When the hope ain't enough
And the freedom bell doesn't ring

Motherhood #1

The noblest gift I'm able to give my daughter
Is to not birth her
Into this world or the next
Not yet, at least, until this world
Prepares itself
To embrace her as wholly human
And let her be
Free

Motherhood #2

I heard them say
That a woman can't raise a boy
To be a man
Then came you
And I knew
Your best hope for survival
In this world of men
Was to be nursed by a mother
Who assumed the agony
Of menfolk

On Womanhood

Virtuous Women

Our mamas said patience is a virtue
Virtuous women are taken first
Well, I'll be last in line
Then
Because I've seen what's on the other side
Of virtue
And I've decided
My life warrants more than
Settling for virile boredom

Untitled #1

If you want to love a 'man'
Don't.
No use wasting your time loving an idea
He doesn't himself understand
Love, instead, the truth
Of Him.

Home Again

She lay down her crown
And picked up mama's Sunday hat
Tattered
Worn
Hers to hold
And heal her head space
And he saw
Her there
…finally

Untitled #2

I cling to pride
In the face of prejudice
Boldly anticipating "No"
Daring to affirm "Yes"
Between pride and prejudice
The choice is only
Survival

I Am Not My Hair

Got a new hairstyle
You couldn't tell the diff'rence
I bought it; it's mine

Chains

My arms are too frail
To lift me up and over your wall
To carry you over your fear

A centuries-old rift
Meet me somewhere in the middle
We are in this together

I will look for you on the other side
And seek a way to know you
And adore you

Notwithstanding your ambition
To compel them see you
As only I can

A Slice of Pie (2009)

My apple pie is sweeter
I use the same cinnamon and nutmeg
The same apples, every time
When you bite into it
Your eyes close
And you relish it with delight
Her pie is peach
And you convince her that you love it
Love her
Just the same
But her peaches are in season
Now, at least
When autumn comes
You come calling
For my sweeter apple pie
And I'm the fool who believes your lies

Dreamer (2013)

The first lesson I learned about boys
Came from one named Tony
His fascination with his dick
Mattered more than my naps
He loved his dick more than he believed in my free will
And he wasn't satisfied until
He could make me feel it
So, he did
And he did
And he did again
Every day
Shhh, be quiet he said
They said
To the four-year-old girl
Who just wanted to dream

Holla

"Damn, baby, you got a fat ass!"

Damn, ugly
Your breath stinks
Your face is fucked up
Your pants are dirty
Your lips are crusty
Your eye is crooked
Your nose got boogers
Your mama should have swallowed
Your daddy should have hugged you
Your mama must have neglected you
Your daddy must have run out on you
Your parents failed you
You need a job
You need a hobby
You need some friends
You need a mentor
You need to leave me alone

Ism

I'm going to shake this table
My aunt demanded a seat
My grandmother served tea
Her father's broken fingers built

I'm going to make a choice
My aunt marched strong
My grandmother brewed bitter herbs
Her father prayed for freedom

I'm going to shatter this ceiling
My aunt poked; cracked
My grandmother wiped clean
Her father could never look up to see

In Protest (2016)

Remember Me

I got a story to tell
Will anyone listen?
I got a story to tell
Can anybody hear me?
I said I got a story to tell
Gotta be somebody out there willing to read it
Because my story is the truth
My story is a long, hard truth
Because my story has a beginning
Middle and it will get to the end
My story ain't for the
Weak stomachs and faint hearts
Gotta be someone out there interested in hearing it
Will someone take a seat at my feet
And pay attention?
My mama named me after someone, I'm sure
Somebody important, gotta be
Because my life had meaning so my name
Must mean something, too
My stomach was weak
All the lead pumped into it
I said my mind took its time
All the lead pumped into it
You listening to me?

My heart skipped four beats
Cop pulled me over
My hands began to sweat
Cop pulled up to my window
I got this story that needs to be told
Because my baby was in the back of my car
They didn't care to look
My baby girl was in the back of my car
Didn't stop them from shooting, though
I know someone out there is hearing me
I only knocked to find help
Stumbling and staggering
I just wanted to tap into some human kindness
But if anyone remembers my story
They know how it ended
And maybe after hearing my story again
Somebody will say my name
Say her name (Korryn)
And her name (Sandra)
And her name (Miriam)
And her name (Renisha)
Somebody... Say her name

Haiku for the Forgotten

Rekia

Tomorrow won't come
A night partying with friends
One shot to the head

Yvette

It was the men's fault
Shot standing in a doorway
Knee-jerk brutality

Aiyana

This child's life stolen
Sleeping through the flash and bang
Makes for great TV

Miriam

Bullet holes riddled
Through car and bodies of two
Mama loved baby

Tanisha

Cuffed on cold pavement
Unraveling mind; disturbed
Breath stolen from life

Sandra

Three days in a cell
Body swinging from where
No answers; no peace

Malissa

Unarmed in a car
One hundred thirty-seven
Wrongful death, they said

Shereese

Family called. "Help!"
Police arrived, providing none
Other than her death

Tarika

Holding her son close
Prey to his fragility
Shots blown in shadows

Korryn

There was a message
She cradled her baby boy
The water's still tainted

Mother's Lament

The lament of a howling mother,
As her first-born son is stolen,
Remains the untold story
Of anguish coursing through a
Cursed woman who should feel no pain
Same as it ever was
The Man, some man
Those men, any men
White then, Black now
Thieves, nonetheless
Her agony no different
Whether noose or bullet
Her burden no easier to bear
Whether owner or brother
No comfort exists for a howling mother
Innumerable stories of unknown children
A mother's screams silence the room
And those who come to pay respects
Silently filed into the small, dank parlor
Moaned "Amen"s, incessant tears
Make amends, a preacher cheers
"There's joy on the other side!"
But sorrow came yesterday morning
The wretched sorrow of a mother's mourning
There will be no justice
After centuries of no peace

I Believed in Freedom (2014)

I believed in Freedom, once.
I heard the muffled rhythm of waves crashing and
Was assailed by the putrid aroma of souls exiting
Disintegrated dwellings.
I tasted the salt of the seas and tears
And mastered escape into
The corners of my mind they could not penetrate—
Unlike my body.
I waited for Freedom to reach the shores before I did
And declare this journey finished and me released.
Instead, I found myself bound;
Found myself… in bondage.
I found Freedom to be a fair-weather friend
And the skies above me wore perpetual clouds.

I believed in Freedom, twice.
I heard the hiss of hatred piercing flesh and
Was agonized, bearing witness to blood departing
Contorted carcasses;
I wiped clean their brows of sweat and eyes of tears.
I mastered his language through my songs—
Lyrics he could never sing.
I begged for Freedom to emancipate us all
And recognize my humanity because
I found myself already human.
I was a human being… in bondage;
I soon learned Freedom was reserved
For those who could afford the bill.

I believed in Freedom, again.
I heard the padding of weary feet marching
Down muddied, bloodied streets, counting and collecting
The souls of the lost, sacrificed;
I cried out in shouts of protest and shed rebellious tears.
I mastered the chants and healed myself,
Inhaled escape plans, shadowboxed my wary self.
I demanded Freedom be given to us—
Loud and proud, I said it.
I was there… in bondage;
I wrote a book about Freedom,
The Impossible Dream.

I believe in Freedom, finally.
I heard 41 shots ring out, 50 shots, 8 shots
Pumped into defenseless limbs of imaginary Black monsters,
Hands up, begging for a few more minutes.
I type their names, replaying videos of mothers' tears
I master the acts of resistance not yet tested
And escape the allure of manufactured solidarity.
I understand Freedom must be taken;
Everything I have been given is rotted with disease.
Freedom has been in bondage—
Bound by circumstance and tribulation…
Awaiting the liberation of Me

The Formula

I experimented with form over the years—Villanelle and Pantoum. I find that working in form is a disciplinary exercise and sometimes, we need to focus. These are a few of the pieces I've come up with.

What You Can't Have (2004)

On vulnerable hearts, tortured souls do prey
The weak move to fight, determined not to break
Emotions have a tendency of getting in the way

Beginning the journey, intertwined, glistening bodies do lay
Fear in their eyes, emotions for each other they cannot fake
On vulnerable hearts, tortured souls do prey

Headed in opposite directions, they beg each other to stay
Fearing separation, but togetherness being what neither can take
Emotions have a tendency of getting in the way

He seeks Her, the epitome of Woman, yet She may
Slip through his fingers; claim he does not allow her to stake
On vulnerable hearts, tortured souls do prey

Making his way through life's clutter, he struggles day-to-day
Repeatedly losing everything, no sense of it can he make
Emotions have a tendency of getting in the way

For sweet salvation, mourners cry out and pray
Love has died; Misery smiles, seated at the Wake
On vulnerable hearts, tortured souls do prey
Emotions have a tendency of getting in the way

Confusion (2004)

My strength evaporates from within, leaving this spirit weak
Questioning if every lie absorbed by my mind over time is true
Seeking peace, listening to revolutionaries speak

A nation of millions; at a glance, destinies appear bleak
Shackled to walls, no sign of freedom within our myopic view
My strength evaporates from within, leaving this spirit weak

Wars waged between brick and concrete street murals; havoc wreaks
Street soldiers on the corners, desperate for something more to do
Seeking peace, listening to revolutionaries speak

Walk through doors of holy dwellings, comforted by peace as a pastor
speaks
Are we not to be better protected, seated in the red, velvet-covered pews?
My strength evaporates from within, leaving this spirit weak

We turn to those innocents. A return to innocence we seek
While exploring abused sexuality; yet find that their numbers are few
Seeking peace, listening to revolutionaries speak

In gracious piety, I utter words in dark closets; blessed are the meek
Burned by need to be more like, existing in fear of…You
My strength evaporates from within, leaving this spirit weak
Seeking peace, listening to revolutionaries speak

God (2005)

I believed God turned His back on me
It all began when I was eleven
I struggled with members of my family
While He silently watched from heaven

It began when I was eleven
That I slowly began to lose my mind
While He silently watched from heaven
My whole sense of being began to unwind

I slowly began to lose my mind
I wanted nothing more than to die
My whole sense of being began to unwind
When I woke up each morning, I would cry

I wanted nothing more than to die
One day I decided to run away
When I woke up each morning, I would cry
I decided my life should not be that way

One day I decided to run away
Seeking refuge in any place but home
I decided my life should not be that way
I knew I would be better off alone

Seeking refuge in any place but home
No longer trusting in God and the lies
I knew I would be better off alone

It was God I began to despise
I no longer trusted in God and His lies
I asked "How could you let this happen to me?"
It was my God who I began to despise
It was as if He left me alone…He simply let me be

I asked, "How could you let this happen to me?"
No child deserves such pain and suffering
It was as if He left me alone…simply leaving me be
All I needed was love, peace, and comforting

No child deserves such pain and suffering
In that suffering, I was blind to the light
All I needed was love, peace, and comforting
And deliverance from my tortured plight

In that suffering, I was blinded by the light
He decided to rescue and save me from darkness
He delivered me from my tortured plight
I understood then, that my existence was never meaningless

He decided to rescue and save me from darkness
God has a plan for me in His world
I know now that my existence was never meaningless
I am a faithful woman, gone is the tortured girl

God has a plan for me in His world
I no longer struggle with my family
I am a woman of faith, no longer a tortured girl
Who believed God turned His back on me…

What I Thought I Knew About Love

Whisper

In the quiet of the night
A whistle in the wind
Carries secrets from lips to ears to hearts
From souls
Feelings untold
It is there in that whispering wind
That Love exists, hidden in the open.
Obvious.
Boldly timid.
Unwavering… consistent.
True.
Wind that whispers to you was once air that I (blew).
(Carrying) Love
(From me to) You.

Labor (Haiku)

I believe in you
Believe your soul's ambition
Don't leave me behind

Untitled #3

She sees
Behind the curtain, sincerity
Good intentions diverted and fulfilled
Sincerely
Hope rests, having taken its residence behind the red shade
A world of change on the horizon
Awaiting its anointed leader
To fulfill His fated destiny
To be more and do more than He understands
He knows, He believes, He succeeds
He endures, He questions, He fears
She hears
Sincerity
Faith exists, sustained in the depths of purple hearts
The horizon of the world is going to change
Waiting patiently
The people need their leaders
To embody their purposes
And do more, be more than they know
She feels, she connects, she dreams
She's suffered, she's doubted, she's shed tears
He sees
Behind the lines, Love
He welcomes, she provides
She invites, He guides
They dance together in the fields of battle
Shielding each other from the onslaught of humanity
They believe
...in truth
...in the possibilities
...in each other

70107942R00021

Made in the USA
Middletown, DE
12 April 2018